URBAN MYTHS AND LEGENDS

D1340210

Urban Myths and Legends

POEMS ABOUT TRANSFORMATIONS

EDITED BY RACHEL PIERCEY AND EMMA WRIGHT

With poems from Deborah Alma, Sophie F Baker, Sohini Basak, Dzifa Benson, Nisha Bhakoo, Rohan Chhetri, Ellie Danak, Francine Elena, Ella Frears, Linda Goulden, John Greening, Jack Houston, Annie Katchinska, Anna Kisby, Joe Lines, Emma McKervey, Margot Myers, Richard O'Brien, Rachel Piercey, Kathy Pimlott, Susan Richardson, Jennifer Robertson, Jacqueline Saphra, Paul Stephenson, Degna Stone, Jon Stone, Pam Thompson, Ruth Wiggins, Ashley Williams and Lana Faith Young

THE EMMA PRESS

I.M. MYFANWY GIDDINGS

THE EMMA PRESS

First published in Great Britain in 2016
by the Emma Press Ltd

ISBN 978-1-910139-24-0

A CIP catalogue record of this book
is available from the British Library.

Printed and bound in Great Britain
by TJ International, Padstow.

The Emma Press
theemmapress.com
queries@theemmapress.com
Birmingham, UK

CONTENTS

LIST OF ILLUSTRATIONS

INTRODUCTION

When I first read Ovid's *Metamorphoses,* about ten years ago, I remember being dazzled by how all the stories were strung together. Every myth's ending provides the starting point for the next and there are sub-stories within the stories, and sometimes sub-sub-stories within those too. The sheer fun of it is intoxicating.

I read the *Metamorphoses* again recently and I was more struck by how horrible most of the stories are – all of them, in fact, if you're disturbed by the idea of being turned into a bird, tree or constellation even as an act of kindness. It's a relentless catalogue of punishment, rape and lamentation, but still Ovid contrives to make it one hell of a ride. He whisks the reader from one myth to the next, telling his tales with relish and moving us along from each tragic outcome with ironic asides.

Part of me finds this callous. But, equally, last week I leant out of a first-floor café window to watch a fight break out on the street below, and I gave a running commentary to the people behind us who couldn't see. 'She's pulled a pointy bit of fence out of her car! She's waving it! The other one's thrown a ketchup bottle! It's gone everywhere! Now her Uber's arrived!'

When Rachel and I put out the call for poems for *Urban Myths and Legends*, we wanted to find poems which shared Ovid's glee in storytelling. We wanted poems with transformations, as a direct link to the *Metamorphoses*, but we also wanted gripping stories which we could imagine being retold and passed on. I wanted this book to evoke the thrill of hearing gruesome stories at school, where everyone seemed to know someone who'd leant backwards on their chair and cracked their head open, or sneezed with their eyes open and their eyeballs popped out, or scratched a spot on their neck and baby spiders poured out.

As it turns out, quite a few of the poems in this book are gruesome, but I think the overall tone is one of curiosity rather than callousness. Where Ovid tends to tell the stories of his transformations at a cool narrator's distance, many of the poets in this book have, instead, sensitively inhabited the voices of the transformed. Transformation in Ovid is sometimes a reward, mostly a punishment and occasionally an act of mercy: it invariably occurs in the context of sexual pursuit, sacrilegious hubris, or, if you're unlucky, both. I'm proud of the diversity of approaches to the theme gathered here. Without losing the Ovidian qualities of fun and surprise, these poets offer something beyond a whistlestop tour of strange tales: a variety of thoughtful perspectives on what transformation might mean today.

Emma Wright
BIRMINGHAM
May 2016

URBAN MYTHS AND LEGENDS

One of Those Things

At some point last week
the swans began to fly
backwards.

That was the week
the scratches on my back
disappeared beneath your fingernails.

The week
I coughed up my tears and took
back a bruise with the heel of my hand

and my jumper unraveled
and my breasts shrank and puckered
and the house began to dismantle itself.

We stood in the garden
holding hands
as the branches swallowed the blossom.

MY PEOPLE

were once human like me

then their bones grew too long for their feet

poked out like spokes
of broken umbrellas

and their lips stretched into snarls
which covered half their face

and those who lived near the canal
grew scales

and those who lived on the tops
grew fur to keep out biting winds

and some sprouted wings
to hunt for food

or so my mother told me
before her toes pitched her

into a middle kingdom
of sloughed-off skins
and reheated dinners.

The Foundling

When we heard him cry out from the dark garden
we thought he was a bird or the wind nagging the gate.
He insisted; we went to check.
A form slumped in the grass, eyes agog,
his flaring ears; how thin he was,
and russet in the kitchen light.
He ran across the floor
and beneath the sofa like a draught.

We knocked on doors and rang the RSPCA
but no one was missing a puppy.
At first he was wary in our bright corridors
but in time he settled. We called him Ben.
He loitered on the edges of our routine,
dozing on the carpet, angling for scraps.
His tail swelled, soot flexed through his fur.
I'd cradle him, then with a jolt
his long limbs would spider
and turn him inside out.

We let him stretch his legs across the football pitch:
his shy, intent stumble, the way the other dogs
would snarl. He never barked back.
One day he bolted across a ditch
and sat on the opposite bank, watching us.
An old lady came by. Eyeing him, she said
that one of them had been sniffing around her bins,
and weren't they getting very fearless – and
wasn't that one very tame?

Double Yellow

He drops his pad. His badged cap
falls from his head. I watch the hardness

of his stare soften, the grey flecks
at his temples darken, the faint wrinkles

at the corners of his eyes plump up.
And now he's shrinking, getting smaller,

falling to his bum. His uniform
starts folding round the feet

that he no longer stands on.
He screams. And as the boozy smell

of fresh colostrum fills his breath,
his ticket's been forgotten. I scoop

him up into my arms.
Dear oh dear oh dear, what's this now?

SALT

after *The Vegetarian*, Han Kang

We sit at the table passing around the blame.
No one takes a slice. An animal tries to warn
us, but we have her for dinner. We were hungry.
Tomorrow we will warm up the leftovers.
We wait for water. A few hours without it
is terrible but we have been told that the body
will adjust. For now, a sandstorm in the throat
but later certain, like bark. One of us is convinced
that she is no longer an animal. More veins, less
blood. We avoid looking at the tall glass with stems
of cut flowers. Unseasonal heat. Our impatient children
stick their fingers into the peach to prize out a stone.
A centre so hard you'd feel lucky to find rings instead
of ribs and where her toes were before, a complication
of roots. Shoot nothing from your mouth but a calm
that confirms not all rainfall is benediction. Imagine
this: a sanitary kitchen, windows, tiles, spoons made
of wood and a row of potted plants, stomata sparkling
like salt. That dawn was chlorophyll stained. Her
wants become simpler: air, liquid, light. No, don't
imagine this; become a paradox so clean it cannot
be touched. Let us compare the sharpness of wives.
We have not come far, it is the forest that recedes
farther away from our reach. Another animal tries
to warn us, we can feel our teeth growing warm. Our
reluctance goes cold. Afterwards, we will paint our grief.

Own Your Days

Own your cracked sink, your shredded hand,
your husband's bouquet of bandages, your hand
gushing into the sink.

Own your knuckles' wintery sting,
your book of poems on *hunger & want,*
your tongue drenched with glycerol.

Own Waterloo,
your bitchy river, quietly somewhere
your Agnus Dei, your elbows elbowing other elbows,

the sculptures of mental health unit patients,
your lump reaction, your raggedy pulse. Own your Sunday,
starchy, clipped –

your tourists, your tower, your Remembrance,
your standard annual response and your cluster
of smartphones buffering, clicking, your air slashed

with instant scripture, whim.
Own each step step step
to her, your stranger of Eastcheap, her books –

your spiralbound WHAT IS HEAVEN, your pocketsize
TESTAMENT, your folded sheet WE CHOOSE JOY,
your postcard DAMASCUS.

Own your mentor's sunflower voice
Do you have any aches or pains,
her eyes like cups of lemonade, your tongue

softer, wetter – own your sudden fluffy tail
and hunger, in your floppy ears her
higher frequency mutter,

your tongue growing
longer, rolling out of your mouth –
now own your needs – your curiosities –

your first bark
Can he fill my wolfish heart –
and own your drooly first decision,

your scent-crazed decision,
your stab-of-a-stick-on-the-collar
decision, on your knees, your pavement,

your four blonde legs –
your mentor's moisturised hand
grabbing, squeezing your split red paw.

Signified

I wear my signifiers bone-deep
and powder-deep. I keep my hair long.
I swear with one eye
on the peripheral company
and wrestle with being sweet.
Today I slipped into a rose.
Romantic people pulled
on my stem and sank their noses
into my cool creases. My thorns
spilt comparisons and my clammy,
layered heart could well
have been crossed with canker.
Today I slipped into a fox.
I was where the town gave onto
the woods; I slunk into the trees
like groundwater. I was the scourge
of hens: farmers rose at dawn
to find necks bent and the brood
too shocked for eggs. Halfway
between wolf and waif:
don't trust me with your child,
your secrets or your grapes.
Today I slipped into my skin
and my familiar symbols.
My long hair felt good;
my pretty dresses fit like a faithful dress.
People knew what to expect.
My skin fit like water over my head.

My Brown-Eyed Girl

This winter, in our forties,
chatting over the washing up,
my sister and I discovered
that she'd always coveted
my grey green eyes
and I, hers of golden brown,
and *Don't It Make My Brown Eyes*
was never personal enough.

So we swapped, we popped out
our eyeballs, slipped them
into our mouths to moisten them
before slotting into familial sockets.
Then we sat down with a nice pot of tea,
lemon drizzle cake
and little chance of rejection.

The story was in *Chat, The News of the World*
and everywhere we looked.
And now I can see
Crystal Gale sings to me
and Van Morrison never stops.

Telescope

On clear nights,
not a stone-throwing youth in sight,
Diabetic Fred to our left
kicks out legs, extends the neck
of his own contraption: a miraculous,
mechanical, mongrel invention
concocted from left-behind lenses –
an all-nighter leaning over,
rifling, torching, welding, fitting,
the bare bulb dangling.

He knocks using the knocker,
calls us to the pavement
to squint a look, twist until sharp.
We take turns marvelling
in our street's planetarium
at the full button moon
with hairline crack.

Next day on the doorstep
Fred sits in bandaged sandals,
as if nothing cosmic has ever
happened between us, blows
through a descant recorder
to his own tune, with ten fingers,
eight toes and one eye clouding over.

The Sewer Swine

'If you value your fingers, don't be fetching for anything lost down
a drain.' – Anon

The women came in ones, mostly.
   Some lewd, some wild, some blue
     with cold, blue with sickness. Thin, pale
   tributaries, they ran to each other.
Freed by kindness. By instinct.
     By keepers who'd thrown a latch
   for a favour. They made for the river.
Thomasina, Tamsin they called her,
   the closest they had to a leader.
     Tall in the shallows, fishing
for pale-footed cray. Always hungry,
   they'd watch her. At dusk, as they'd settle
     on cold, shingle beaches, she'd teach them
   to skim, to make little sow prints
in the glass of the river. Days in,
     and the river grew fatter, less easy,
   the smell of the city in waves. Together,
they swam out to an island.
   A single line of wood smoke, a clearing.
     And in it a man, his name Spencer Seeley.
O he was enchanting, smelt of cedar
   and clove, but his island was startling,
     filled with creatures – wild, but docile.
   Deer nudged them. The women walked on.
They were hungry, they were famished –
     You're half-starved, you poor dears!

From the kitchens, quiet servants appeared.
They made a strange sight, twelve
                in white at his table, wild-haired
                                and weird. Seeley's fingers at play
in a bowl of gold rings. On came
                the soup bowls, porcelain thick
                                with morels. A pie made of cobnuts.
                Fresh apples and chestnuts.
They dined very well. Maud
                                was the first, but the cry went round
                the table: *Let's feast like this for ever,*
on things of the earth! Seeley smiled,
                Well then, I'll take you all at your word.
                                He passed round a jug, filled
with green hops and honey,
                and they each drained a tankard.
                                Moustaches of foam. Giddy,
                they felt a change coming over.
Their bare feet split neat, into hard
                                little hooves. Their rumps bustled
                and thickened, their muscles
grew strong. The fattening,
                the larding, the laying on of pork.
                                Four-square on their trotters,
in a trample of dresses, straight-tailed
                and yard-broomed they stood. And what
                                of their noses? O each was a rose,
                or a posy of phlox. A cinnamon
warehouse, a sloppy wet trough.
                                They could root out a turnip, or trickster
                for sport. And here was a trickster.

Seeley came on, with a ring
for each nose. They gathered, as one.
Said Tamsin, *Did you think we'd be pink?*
Docile little squeakers? Sweet hams
for your plate? Well we're far,
far fiercer. And with that,
they rushed forward to stove
the man in. His last words were
Wait! I can return you!
Return us?! they squealed, *We've already fled!*
What was left of their voices
then quit them. And they swam
to the city, to make its sewer
their wallow. No acorns
down there, but they feast well
on night soil and fingers. And wary
the husband or father who finds them,
the black sows of London.

PORTRAIT : LANDSCAPE

First thing she's a front garden   crisp packet in the cotoneaster
yes   but bright borders   a mix of bedding and hardy annuals.

     By the time the dew has dried on the mossy lawn
she's gone frenchified   euro-metropolitan
                     gravel paths and rows

of strictly perpendicular cypress stretch to her vanishing point.
Her punched metal notices grow sharper
                  as footsteps raise dust.

        By mid-afternoon she's a margin
of alder   yarrow   nettles littered with cans and foxgloves
disappearing   then re-emerging   at each dank tunnel.

At teatime

she's a prospect of hills   mild undulations of cultivated land loped
over by rabbits   on the ridge a spinney sketched against
the sky.

        Around nine   an aerial view reveals the lights
strung along her harbour wall   in her deep-silled cottage windows
                        blinking   on   a   tanker

out at sea.

Ah

    but in those small hours

                she's the Great Steppe.

                        The miles

of her nomadic heartland

                thud to hoof-drummed histories.

LITTLE ALBERT

The rats are on the march again
they chain-gang from the pattern
in the linoleum
tail-to-mouth   ratstring
slide ratpython
in my crib
I am
lost

Dark
a rat
-skin blanket
I can't breathe through
fur   my mouth a nest
I choke and scream out *rats*
and when you carry me free
I burrow your folds   hide my claws

Note: 'Little Albert' was a baby used in a 1920s experiment
to discover if a phobia (fear of rats) could be induced in a
previously healthy child.

Tokyo

In the hot dense matter
which is the breath of this city,
I sometimes tasted pollen in my sleep
and went searching for skirt.

I discovered her in the ditch
of a sleeping highway
riddled with the storms of oil
and the stench of tar.

Athlete, she ran through the metropolis,
the shaving-blade trees,
the constant hours of glass,
all sulking from a neon disease.

In the best chamber of a western hotel
I displayed riches in furnishings,
my love in jewels and polluted champagne.

We wrestled on a mattress
dead as the weight
as the weight I desired.

When a shard of the bed's vertebrae
rose through the elastic of her skin,
it surfaced through the canvas of her back
like a tailor's pin in a new shirt.

Come Undone

'I take pleasure in my transformations. I look quiet and
consistent, but few know how many women there are
in me.' – Anaïs Nin

No more walls, she says.
No more coats. I'll have none of that.
None of your hands
shadow-boxing a hermit crab.
No more repetitive shapes
or sharks to
set things right

ocean after ocean after ocean

I'll speak of things, of names
too difficult to decipher.
And yes, no more changing into a flower,
a sea anemone, a jellyfish.
I'll remember that all animals
are predatory
at the bottom of the sea.

And then I'll speak of
hurricanes, mirrors,
and odd-numbered
fantasies.
And then I'll speak
of a brokenness you call
inadequate, paltry, blonde.

You will not be able to see me change.
You will not see me drifting into the sea.
There will be nothing aquatic
about this shipwreck. You will not know
the colour blue.
When I put stones in my pocket
you'll still be looking at a mermaid

and saying,
Look, how close she is to the ship.

Aisha Kandisha

He was half insane and wanted the other half
all of his life, his feet were sewn in
the Fez medina, the same hiss and cluck
but he wasn't whole, only halfway there,
halfway to a fantasy, away, underwater –

Her face would lick him into crackling sin,
a fish-hook woman, the most alluring jinn
deep inside the river, a razor blade,
her touch would make him majaneen,
her tears would seep into his veins

(A reverse watermelon? A weep bucket?
Blowing kisses into the wind? To a bitch?)

Her beauty would be his thrill,
as she bit into him just like an orange
a sudden star would light her face,
a stain, a cyst, a juice upon the water,
Aisha Kandisha, a repetition on the lips!

But this hoofed woman didn't swallow him,
from whisper to a snore his mouth drowned instead,
it was the call to prayer that finally shook him
and the early half-moon that snatched him away,
took him by the hand, deep into the medina

(He drank dirty water from the well…)

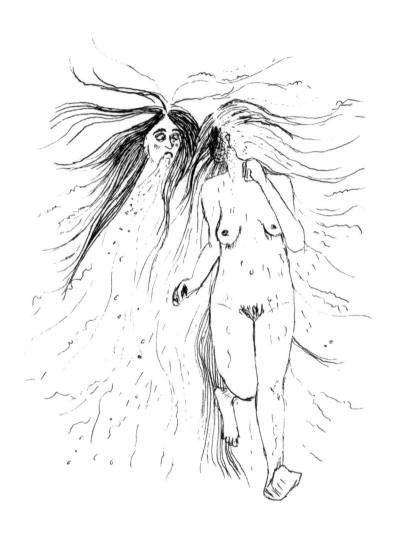

THE MAN ON THE RUNWAY

from *Heath*

A man has been spotted standing on the runway, looking
anxiously as if he were waiting for the Tube, although
the Tube will not be leaving Hounslow for years.
Flights have been grounded, security is on its way,
but he's unmoved, intent on looking, looking
for his briefcase, this best-dressed scarecrow, unscared
by lasers, acoustic dispersal, or high-vis waving
*(Clear off – people are wanting their holidays, there are
urgent supplies for Africa, VIPs
in the lounge, animals in the hold!).* Where is that missing
combination lock, whose number he knows so well
he can repeat it, repeat it…? A honking red
and orange v comes smearing by to flash
and grab the scene, and hisses right through him.

Of course, he was never there. An urban myth
drifting through our online departure lounge,
materialised from something in 1948,
a crash, or some other rubbish from the 70s.

But I knew that man. He walked out on to the Heath
one morning in his grey flared suit,
his sandwiches safe in their Tupperware, and disappeared
into the rising sun, took off, was gone,
his paunch, moustache and sideburns, his cigarette smoke,
and in his briefcase – what? Not, one imagines,
a report on the latest findings regarding the percentage
of people in terminal buildings who might be ghosts.

EAGLE AND CHILD

How can the boy remember?
I never breathed a word.
There were so many children,
my husband said, left crying
in crowded cots and those poor,
exhausted, half-distracted girls
struggling to mind each one.
We couldn't help them all.

At first he hardly ever cried,
stayed silent, sleeping or awake.
His little fists curled closed,
then open, his arms flapping,
his legs kicking, his eyes tracking
me right across the room.
One day (the milk warming)
he made this clucking sound.

When I laughed, he laughed
back at me. Soon he grew
strong, loud, clever, musical.
He knew his sister's stories
word for word, by heart.
Today, he tells his own:
chickens squawk in a hen coop;
a great eagle carries one away.

AQUATIC APE THEORY

The water in my house moves slow:
the bath takes an age to drain,
the cistern an hour to fill,
and each tap drizzles lacklustre
when coffee grains need sweeping away.

I wonder what secret creatures
lurk in the plumbing of my home,
drinking deep of the clean water's flow
and misdirecting the suds with cunning
sleight of hand.

I imagine the landscape Noah beheld
in the Flood's ebbing tide:
the bloated remains of the unsaved
half feasted on by fish, whose gills
may not have been an oversight
but allowed to remain with a managerial eye
on the need for a thorough clean up.

Perhaps some fast-evolving apes
embraced the aquatic to survive
with inter-toe webbing
and prodigious lungs,

who continued to evolve with time
until becoming the clandestine miniature of themselves,
who live in my pipes,
who think I believe myself made in His image
and seek a quiet revenge.

Paper-thin

The day the stile tore at my grandma's leg
I watched how blood looks, pooled
under tracing paper. Haematoma,
they called it, though that doesn't quite cover

how the rest of her bleached. But that
was long before we saw what she'd become.
That took a gathering of layers over years,
while her eyes papered over,

opaque from the drying smudges
on the deckle of her retina. And as we watched
the nurse peel sheets of her tissue-dry lips
with a coarse pink sponge on a plastic stick,

that was most likely the catalyst.
Her death became the act of stripping wallpaper
back: one story at a time, all the way
to a blanched clean sheet none of us recognised

empty of the laid lines of our own thin lives.
How pale, underneath all that, how pale she'd been
with grief. She rustled with the slowing of her paper-bag breaths
as she folded inside her own skin and bled out.

The Tame

The sun pushes her towards the dark waters of the Tame. She doesn't need to be told, she knows if she walks along the river bed she can hold her breath as long as she needs. She reaches the place where the Swans hold court. They dip their heads under the water and speak to her without saying a word. She asks them if she can stay and they don't say no. They tell her they can break a man's neck, if he gets too close.

Scylla

I know she dosed me. A similar name to my own, like
Saoirse circle seashell searching. Older with veined, hitchhiker
arms, batik pants, matted hair, a kind of amulet against
the bones of her chest.

My final night at that beach she bought me a piña colada,
called all men pigs, threw her tarot pack across the bamboo
tables, agitating small clusters of travellers like
mosquitoes near DEET.

Her man approached me, same as before. Fish noodle
breath and scaly hands. I ran to the cool sand and swam in
my shorts like the Thai girls who had told me of
box jellyfish.

A nauseous disturbance near my body, turbulent sea water.
Foaming teeth of thick dogs rising, presa canarios, I saw
their co-joined brutality. A barking part of me,
my own terrifying brain.

DZIFA BENSON

Myself, When I Am Real

'Woman Accidentally Joins Search Party Looking For Herself'

When I was Xetsa, the African Grey, I said:
even if I am bleeding, please look
at my red tail feathers. You'll find I'm still whole.

I was my twin Evi, void and bellyful at the same time.
Raging and hungry as the grey sea,
my throat closed like dough that can't rise.

I was cousin Kafui when every moon was blue.
What was the word going round and round
in my head? I let it dry on me like a wet shirt.

I was loving Afi, despair sitting fat inside, rearing
its jaundiced head. I wasn't lost but I set myself free.
Living loud in my elsewhere, I became the last girl, Mansa.

My mother's voice said 'Remember Noona, a little bit
of purple lipstick changes your day.' I spent my time wishing
I was a wolf with its soft underbelly and big animal gaze.

Now I am Brandina, my great-great grandmother. I spread
myself so thin and green, I am an elephant's back in Phuket,
a beach in Anloga, a discarded shoe in Boston.

Through the wing of a dragonfly, I point to darkness.
Soon I will become Fafali, the youngest.

WHAT I AM REALLY THINKING

father wants me to fill my head with zen   instead of ideas
of soaring   suicide levels are higher among young men
noise is the habit of this world   I want to escape
the roaring outside this door   is no excuse for staying in
I spit out   rage   unable to sit still   to have the guts
to be   this light   lacks strength to cut   through wax
my cross-stitched arms   greenery boosts mental health
in my hand a sparrow a torn-hole wing   I could leave it
terror-stricken   here   for a tomcat   instead I snap
its threadbare neck   the cooling gleam in its eyes
don't look down   I really really ought to get out more
the sparrow   with its last heartbeat   plunging
as we move   towards treetops   I will it to be well
before I

GLASS SHOES

It's the wishbone thinking
that has ladies snapping heels
night after night – eventually
breaking more than glass tongues. Their
flesh-white soles scratch and bleed
and then they're bare toes and stumbling laughter,
which disguises a pained whimper, not
quite held in as they
limp on a friend to a chair.

It's the prince mentality
that thoughtfully returns to a girl
the same killer footwear
that she dropped
the night before last (or at least recently)
because she looks so good in shoes
through which you can see the vague outline
of soot burns and blisters.
The shoe suits her and fits her –
and he is delighted and she
is glad for his kind gaze
which transforms her
from a woman with feet throbbing,
numb as a bucket of water,
to a woman glittering, not with sweat
but something other…

PIECEWORK

Mum is doing piecework in her bedroom. She slaps herself, moans, begs for more. We catch glimpses through the hole punched in the plywood door. Hair in rag rollers, wearing a chewing gum grey t-shirt. Her words dress her in a skinny body, blonde hair trailing down to her waist, nothing but candyfloss panties between her and the caller. Some days it's quality control on stockings, other days stitching shammy leathers.

Each night

he grips the remote
half asleep
at his end of the sofa

surfs
the flickering
forms

that rise
as if from ditch
or hedge

dreams the forest
cleaves

falters

                  she
                  meanwhile

                  the sofa cushion
                  moulded to her hips

                  tuned out years ago

                  dreams

                  of a tangle of briar
                  a stem grown thick as a man's wrist.

LAST HARVEST

So when you said asparagus
I took myself to market,
bought the finest I could find.

I scoured my books for recipes:
Apicius, Mrs Beaton,
Elizabeth David, Raymond Blanc.

I prepared asparagus
for every meal: with foaming
hollandaise, vinaigrette,

green and white with truffles
and without,
oven-roasted in olive oil,

airy in soufflés, liquidised
for soup. I watched for signs
from you as I fed you tips

from a silver spoon: nothing.
You chewed and swallowed
but still you didn't give me

The Look. So I got down
on my knees, staked out
the garden in perfect rows,

raised more asparagus
from seed. I dug
my own furrows, tended,

thinned and weeded till my skin
was the colour of earth.
While you slept, I kept watch

for thieves and creeping things,
and when the plants were ripe,
I fed them all to you.

But soon my crop was gone,
my garden barren;
I laced my boots

and commandeered
allotments to grow more.
I watered my asparagus,

talked to them, stroked
their stems, sprayed
their feathered leaves.

While you languished
fat and hungry in the sun,
I told them my love,

and they grew tall as totems,
beautiful, but you consumed
them all. So I bulldozed

ancient woodlands, cleared
more acres, annexed farms,
killed crops. Cows

had nowhere left to graze.
Wildflowers died.
Still your hunger gnawed at me.

I razed the towns and left
the dispossessed camped out
between rows of asparagus

but still you would not change,
even as I stuffed you with my harvest
till your face turned slowly green.

It was then I bound you –
neck and wrist with strings of berries,
dressed your mouth with yellow petals.

Though you did not speak again
you were alert and growthful
as you ate the light.

Your limbs lengthened, your feet
grew roots. Your season:
I took up my spade and dug

a wide furrow; and there
below my window, the earth
newly turned, I planted you.

YARDANG

The jackal wind is changing me
degree by blundersome degree,
though into what, to what extent
and to what end's beyond the scope
of what I know. I know its reach
is vast, that I'm a striplet-stretch
of beach before its sculpting sweep,
its spindle wail – and so we're clear,
it's me who broke into the vault
and turned it loose, who judged it safe
(well, not exactly), made secure
my grapple line and blew the lock.
Out it came, a tortile bolt
of drunkard wind – dying to screw
and strew, to chew and chisel bone
or stone, to shave down to a hump
each stump. Now I'm a blasted dune,
the scoundrel's plaything. Now I drift,
as darkly as the shifting coast,
from one form to some other, strand
by strand, flayed to my filament,
while on its high and singing wire
the mad sylph speaks its only line.
My faltering's its favourite band,
my knots its little coterie.
The coward wind is changing me.

John the Bear

A wife and husband lay in bed;
They're whispering and kissing;
But by the time that one awoke
The other one was missing.

She shifts and stirs and turns about:
He's nowhere to be found.
There's hair upon the pillowcase.
There's hair upon the ground.

And then she up and follows it:
It is the strangest trail.
The pots and pans have clattered down.
His clothes are in a pile.

And dimly now she knows he groaned;
'I'm going out,' he told her.
There's claw-marks on the kitchen door.
There's marks upon her shoulder.

She's gone into her own backyard;
She's seen a silver beech;
She's seen a dark shape climbing up
Until it's out of reach.

And whether he's been up all night
Or whether he's descended,
She's run into the house again
Before the night has ended.

The doors are all of sturdy oak
And heavy on their hinges,
And every latch is put across
And barred are all the windows,

And though outside he calls and calls,
He scratches and he scrapes,
Without his pretty cotton clothes
He cannot change his shape;

And though he scratches and he scrapes,
He thunders and he bellows,
The clothes that lay upon the floor
Are lying there tomorrow.

And when she heard him scrape and scratch
Did she not know his voice?
Did she forget his other shape,
Or did she make a choice?

The clothes are cold upon the floor,
The hair is swept away,
And by the time he hears the broom
He can no longer stay.

The doors are all of sturdy oak,
The walls of sturdy plaster;
And he could be a man again
For all that it would matter.

FROM *SKINDANCING*

'... Sometimes they were people / and sometimes animals / and there was no difference.' – words spoken by Nalungiaq, from *The Netsilik Eskimos* by Knud Rasmussen

If it wasn't for the chill
I still equate with getting naked.

If it wasn't for the way he fixates
on my hair – *Awesome colour,*
d'you henna it?

If it wasn't for the absurdity of skirts –
trailing, but failing to swish like a tail.

If it wasn't for the yipping litters of words
I must birth and nurture daily.

If it wasn't for how my stealth
unnerves him – *Christ, you made me jump,*
I didn't hear you come in.

If it wasn't that risotto's
no substitute for voles.

If it wasn't for having to scavenge
for apt emotions,
in bin bags crammed with irony
and scraps of shame.

If it wasn't for the tyranny
of being upright.

EXPULSION FROM EDEN

from 'Variations on the Homeric Simile'

Like the way we sometimes wake up
devastated from a morning dream

with a heaviness like a fossil of the soft
animal we were, & for a moment we rage

in our beds in disbelief, unable to put down
the terminal roil of that originless terror.

How we're inconsolable,
inconsolable for that brief moment

when the other world still holds us
in a long, incomprehensible grief.

As you go through life

There will be intersecting roads that once were rivers
that once were fathers crying for daughters lost or fallen.

There will be seed-heads in meadows ripe
for blowing that were, at some point, stolen brides.

There will be spaces that whisper *church* to you:
an orchard, an empty football ground, a library, a teacher's car.

There will be snow.
An open flower a shade of certain blue that claims

to take the shape of God. You know the family across the road
were birds before they moved here? The boiled egg

you cracked this morning was not a boiled egg
but a yellow sun-rise ocean, though the toast you dipped

was toast. You've seen your father bristle from man to walrus,
your mother disappear into a crystal tumbler,

you know that if you're ever chased by men or dogs
you'll stretch your fingers upwards, think of leaves.

You've seen them, those little flashes of light in your vision
falling from old moons trapped in lightbulbs. But darling,

those angels that you see in bathrooms over too-hot water,
through steam, are always your own pink limbs descending.

SUPERSTITION

I never actually thought I was knocking
the devil off my shoulder
with a pinch of spilled salt,
but the motion
made me feel I belonged somehow,
my small gesture tying me to
the small gestures of many years
that my grandmothers may have made.
Maybe all that salt we've tossed
has been stacking up,
rebuilding a scattered saline pillar,
and some day if my daughter dares to look behind
she will see it transformed once again
into a complete woman.

ACKNOWLEDGEMENTS

'Brown-Eyed Girl', by Deborah Alma, was first published in her pamphlet *True Tales of the Countryside* (Emma Press, 2015).

'Scylla', by Francine Elena, was first published in *Poetry Wales* in 2015.

'Eagle and Child', by Linda Goulden, was first published in 2014 in Manchester Cathedral's 'Writing The Cathedral' anthology.

'The Man on the Runway', by John Greening, first appeared in his collaboration with Penelope Shuttle, *Heath* (Nine Arches, 2016).

'from *skindancing*', by Susan Richardson, was first published in her collection *skindancing* (Cinnamon Press, 2015).

'Come Undone', by Jennifer Robertson, was first published in *The Missing Slate* in February 2016.

'Last Harvest', by Jacqueline Saphra, was first published in her collection *The Kitchen of Lovely Contraptions* (flipped eye, 2011).

'Telescope', by Paul Stephenson, was previously published in his pamphlet *Those People* (Smith/Doorstop, 2015).

ABOUT THE POETS

Deborah Alma has an MA in Creative Writing, teaches at Worcester University and works with people with dementia and at the end of their lives using poetry. She is Emergency Poet in her 1970s ambulance and edited *Emergency Poet: An Anti-Stress Anthology*. Her debut pamphlet is *True Tales of the Countryside* (Emma Press, 2015).

Sophie F Baker has had work published in magazines including *Smiths Knoll, The Rialto, Poetry London* and *Magma*. She has an Andrew Waterhouse Award from New Writing North, and an Eric Gregory Award. She works at The Poetry Society and is a founding editor of poetry magazine *Butcher's Dog*. www.sophiefbaker.co.uk

Sohini Basak lives and works in Delhi. She was one of the recipients of the inaugural RædLeaf India Poetry Prize and was shortlisted for the 2014 Melita Hume Poetry Prize. She is a recent graduate of the University of East Anglia, where she was awarded the Malcolm Bradbury Continuation Grant for Poetry.

Dzifa Benson was born in London to Ghanaian parents and grew up in West Africa. She writes, performs, curates and teaches, and has performed her work at venues including Tate Britain, the Institute of Contemporary Arts and Southbank Centre. She was a writer-in-residence at the Courtauld Institute of Art in 2007-8.

Nisha Bhakoo is a writer based in Berlin. Her poetry has appeared in *3:AM Magazine, Haverthorn*, Mud Press's *Christmas Zine, Poems In Which* and *Ink Sweat and Tears*. In 2015, she was shortlisted for the Jane Martin Poetry Prize, won third prize in the Ledbury Festival competition and was selected for the GlogauAIR artist residency scheme.

Rohan Chhetri is a Nepali-Indian poet. His poems have been published in *Eclectica, Rattle, EVENT* and *The Antigonish Review*, among others, and is forthcoming in *Prelude* and *Fulcrum*. He has won The (Great) Indian Poetry Collective's 'Emerging Poets Prize 2015', and his first book of poems, *Slow Startle*, will be published in July 2016.

Ellie Danak is an Edinburgh-based poet with a background in researching Swedish crime novels. Her poems have been published in a number of anthologies and magazines, including the Emma Press, *Magma, Antiphon* and others. She is on the Scottish Book Trust's New Writers Awards 2016 shortlist.

Francine Elena was born in Canterbury and grew up in London, Portugal and Scotland. Her poems were shortlisted for the 2014 PigHog Prize and have appeared in various publications including *The Best British Poetry* 2013 and 2015 anthologies, the *Sunday Times, Poetry London, Poetry Wales, The Quietus, Ambit, 3:AM Magazine* and *Wasafiri*.

Ella Frears has had poetry published in *Lighthouse, Poems In Which, The Stockholm Review of Literature* and *The Moth*, among others. She is a trustee of *Magma* and is co-editing issue 66. She was shortlisted for Young Poet Laureate for London (2014) and was Poet in Residence at Knole House (2015). Ella is currently a Jerwood/Arvon Mentee (2016/17).

Linda Goulden alternates between urban and rural settings and her poems between magazine (incl. *Magma*), anthology (incl. Beautiful Dragons), digital (incl. Fair Acre) and readings (incl. Sheffield Poem-a-thon). Her poem in this book was first published by Manchester Cathedral, where you will find a wood carving of the Eagle and Child.

John Greening is a winner of the Bridport and TLS Prizes and a Cholmondeley Award and an RLF Writing Fellow at Newnham College, Cambridge. His recent books include *To the War Poets* (Carcanet), the music anthology *Accompanied Voices,* and *Heath* (with Penelope Shuttle) from Nine Arches Press. See www.johngreening.co.uk

Although they recently had to neuter Ralph, their dog, after he got into one too many fights, **Jack Houston** and his partner have had a baby so don't feel so bad about it. His recent work can be found online at *London Grip, The London Journal of Fiction* and *New Boots & Pantisocracies.*

Annie Katchinska was born in Moscow in 1990 and grew up in London. Her Faber New Poets pamphlet was published in 2010, and her poems have been published in various journals and anthologies. After graduating from Cambridge University she spent two years living in Sapporo, Japan, before returning to London in 2013.

Anna Kisby is a Devon-based poet widely published in magazines and anthologies, including *Magma, Mslexia, Poetry News,* the British Library's Alice anthology and Live Canon's Project 154: contemporary poets respond to Shakespeare's sonnets. She was commended in the Faber New Poets Scheme 2016.

Joe Lines studied English at the University of Sussex and Queen's University Belfast. His poems have appeared in *Causeway/Cabhsair, The Cadaverine* magazine and *The Lifeboat.*

Emma McKervey studied at Dartington College of Arts and lives in Northern Ireland. She has worked in community arts and education over the years and has had numerous poems published in journals and anthologies.

Margot Myers lives in Oxford. She loves using myth and fairytale in her poetry. She has been placed or commended in The Havant Poetry Competition 2013, 2014 and 2015, the Cinnamon Press mini-competition Feb 2016, and shortlisted for The Bridport Flashfiction Prize 2015. She has a poem in *The Emma Press Anthology of Dance* (2015).

Richard O'Brien's pamphlets include *The Emmores* (Emma Press, 2014) and *A Bloody Mess* (Valley Press, 2015). His work has featured in *Oxford Poetry, Poetry London*, and *The Salt Book of Younger Poets*. He is working on a Midlands3Cities-funded PhD on Shakespeare and verse drama at the University of Birmingham.

Kathy Pimlott's poems have been published in magazines including *Magma, Brittle Star* and *The North,* online and in anthologies, most recently the Emma Press's *Best Friends Forever*. In 2015, she was one of the Poetry Trust's Aldeburgh Eight. Her pamphlet *Goose Fair Night* was published in March 2016 by the Emma Press.

Susan Richardson is a Welsh poet, performer and educator. Her third poetry collection, *skindancing* (Cinnamon Press, 2015), is themed around human-animal metamorphosis and our intimacy with, and alienation from, the wild and our animal selves. She is currently poet-in-residence with both the Marine Conservation Society and World Animal Day.

Jennifer Robertson is a poet and critic living in Bombay. Her book reviews and essays have appeared in *Scroll, American Book Review* and the *Telegraph*. She co-curates the 'Literary Encounters' session for The PEN-All India Centre. Her first poetry manuscript was chosen for the Editor's choice award by The (Great) Indian Poetry Collective.

Jacqueline Saphra's *The Kitchen of Lovely Contraptions* (flipped eye) was nominated for the Aldeburgh First Collection Prize. *If I Lay on my Back I Saw Nothing but*

Naked Women (Emma Press) won Best Collaborative Work at the Saboteur Awards 2015. Her second collection, *All My Mad Mothers*, is due from Nine Arches Press in Spring 2017.

Paul Stephenson was a winner in the Poetry Business Book & Pamphlet Competition, judged by Billy Collins. His pamphlet *Those People* (Smith/Doorstop) was published in 2015. He has been published in magazines including *The Rialto, The North* and *Magma*. He took part in the Jerwood/Arvon mentoring scheme. He currently lives in Paris.

Degna Stone is a poet and producer based in Tyne and Wear. She is co-founder of *Butcher's Dog* poetry magazine and in 2015 she received a Northern Writers Award. She was recently selected for The Complete Works III, a national development programme for advanced Black and Asian poets.

Jon Stone is a commissioning editor at Sidekick Books and a PhD researcher in poetry-game hybrids. His collection *School of Forgery* (Salt, 2012) was a PBS Recommendation and he won the Poetry London competition in 2014. His latest pamphlet is *Tomboys* (Tungsten Press, 2016), a set of calligrams based on inspiring girl characters from anime.

Pam Thompson is a poet and university lecturer based in Leicester. She is one of the organisers of Word!, a spoken-word night at The Y Theatre and her publications include *The Japan Quiz* (Redbeck Press, 2009) and *Show Date and Time* (Smith/Doorstop, 2006). She won First Prize (Judges' Prize) in the Magma Poetry Competition in 2015.

Ruth Wiggins lives in London. Her work has appeared in magazines and anthologies, and her first pamphlet *Myrtle* was published by the Emma Press in 2014. She blogs about poetry, travel and mud at mudpath.wordpress.com

Lana Faith Young lives in Australia. In 2012 Lana was shortlisted for the Western Australian Premiere's Book Awards in the digital narrative category. Lana has recently completed a Bachelor of Communications degree through Griffiths University. Lana is currently writing her second novel for children.

ABOUT THE EDITORS

Rachel Piercey is a poet and editor who also writes for children. Her poems have appeared in magazines including *Magma, The Rialto, Poems In Which, Butcher's Dog* and *The Poetry Review* and she has two pamphlets with the Emma Press, *The Flower and the Plough* and *Rivers Wanted*.

Emma Wright studied Classics at Brasenose College, Oxford. She worked in ebook production at Orion Publishing Group before leaving to set up the Emma Press in 2012. In 2015 she toured the UK with the Myths and Monsters poetry tour for children, supported with funding from Arts Council England as part of the Lottery-funded Grants for the Arts programme. She lives in Birmingham.

THE EMMA PRESS

small press, big dreams

The Emma Press is an independent publisher dedicated to producing beautiful, thought-provoking books. It was founded in 2012 by Emma Wright in Winnersh, UK, and is now based in Birmingham. It was shortlisted for the Michael Marks Award for Poetry Pamphlet Publishers in both 2014 and 2015.

In 2015 we travelled around the country with Myths and Monsters, a tour of poetry readings and workshops aimed at children aged 9-12. This was made possible with a grant from Grants for the Arts, supported using public funding by the National Lottery through Arts Council England.

Our current publishing programme includes themed poetry anthologies for adults and children and single-author poetry and prose pamphlets, with an ongoing engagement with the works of the Roman poet Ovid. We publish books which excite us and we are often on the lookout for new writing.

Sign up to the monthly Emma Press newsletter to hear about our events, publications and upcoming calls for submissions. All of our books are available to buy from our online shop, as well as to order or buy from all good bookshops.

http://theemmapress.com
http://emmavalleypress.blogspot.co.uk/

A Poetic Primer for Love and Seduction

Edited by Rachel Piercey and Emma Wright
Series: The Emma Press Ovid
RRP £10 / ISBN 978-0-9574596-3-2

An anthology of instructional poems by modern poets dispensing advice on love, seduction, relationships and heartbreak, channelling the spirit of Roman poet Ovid.

Homesickness and Exile

Poems about Longing and Belonging

Edited by Rachel Piercey and Emma Wright
Series: The Emma Press Ovid
RRP £10 / ISBN 978-1-910139-02-8

How does it feel to be a foreigner? Can you choose where you call home? *Homesickness and Exile* is a collection of poems about the fundamental human need to belong to a place.

Mildly Erotic Verse

Edited by Rachel Piercey and Emma Wright
Series: The Emma Press Anthologies
RRP £10 / ISBN 978-1-910139-34-9

Mildly Erotic Verse skips the mechanics and dives straight into the emotional core of sex, celebrating the diversity and eccentricity of human sexuality.

THE EMMORES, by Richard O'Brien

Series: The Emma Press Picks
RRP £5 / ISBN 978-0-9574596-4-9

Richard O'Brien deploys every trick in the love poet's book in this irresistible mix of tender odes, introspective sonnets, exuberant free verse and anthems of sexual persuasion.

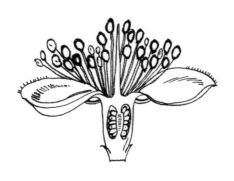

MYRTLE, by Ruth Wiggins

With an introduction by Deryn Rees-Jones
Series: The Emma Press Pamphlets
RRP £6.50 / ISBN 978-1-910139-05-9

In her debut pamphlet, Ruth Wiggins celebrates the primal forces of nature and the human heart. Interweaving the ancient with the modern world, she explores fertility and death, in poems imbued with a subtle eroticism.

GOOSE FAIR NIGHT

By Kathy Pimlott
With an introduction by Clare Pollard
Series: The Emma Press Pamphlets
RRP £6.50 / ISBN 978-1-910139-35-6

Goose Fair Night is a generous, jellied feast of a book, full of sharp-eyed yet tender details about friendship, family and familiarity.

DISSOLVE TO: L.A.

Series: The Emma Press Picks
By James Trevelyan
RRP £5 / ISBN 978-1-910139-37-0

110 x 178 mm / 36 pages / 12 poems / 9 illustrations

What does it mean to die in a movie scene? To exist on the peripheries? James Trevelyan takes twelve cult action films of the 1980s and 90s and gives life where it was extinguished too early.

AWOL

By John Fuller and Andrew Wynn Owen,
with colour illustrations by Emma Wright
Series: Art Squares
RRP £12.50 / ISBN 978-1-910139-28-8

In rural Wales, John Fuller has composed a letter on the subject of travel: warning against it, and wondering about people's presences and absences. Andrew Wynn Owen replies with enthusiasm, matching John's poetic form while hopping from gallery to garret.

Malkin, by Camille Ralphs

Series: The Emma Press Picks

RRP £5 / ISBN 978-1-910139-30-1

Malkin brims and bubbles with the voices of those accused in
the Pendle Witch Trials of 1612. Thirteen men and women
– speaking across the centuries via Ralphs' heady use of free
spelling – plead, boast and confess, immersing the reader in this
charged and dangerous time in history.

True Tales of the Countryside, by Deborah Alma

With an introduction by Helen Ivory

RRP £6.50 / ISBN 978-1-910139-26-4

Deborah Alma writes vividly about sex, love and ageing in rural
Shropshire and Wales, reflecting on her experiences as a mixed-
race, British-Asian woman.

BEST FRIENDS FOREVER: POEMS ABOUT FEMALE
FRIENDSHIP, edited by Amy Key

RRP £10 / ISBN 978-1-910139-07-3

The idea of the best friend defines the social and emotional lives of
many young girls and continues to have an impact into adulthood,
even as The One BFF relaxes into many close female friendships.
Best Friends Forever is a celebration of the transformative power of
this frequently overlooked and misunderstood relationship.

IF I LAY ON MY BACK I SAW NOTHING BUT NAKED WOMEN

By Jacqueline Saphra, with colour illustrations by Mark Webber
Series: Art Squares

RRP £12.50 / ISBN 978-1-910139-06-6

A sumptuous sequence of prose poems about the eccentric
activities of parents and step-parents, as seen from a child's
perspective. The poems are illustrated with linocuts which celebrate
real bodies and complement the vivid atmosphere.